SERPENT HUSBANDRY

A Comprehensive Guide to Snake Farming

BOOK 1

David Nkem

Copyright © 2023 David Nkem

For permission requests, contact the publisher at dnkem048@gmail.com.

Table of Content

Introduction to Snake Farming

In a quaint village nestled between rolling hills, lived a young man named Liam. Liam had always been fascinated by snakes since he was a child. His curiosity about these enigmatic creatures had only grown stronger over the years. However, growing up in a village far from any educational institutions or mentors, he had limited resources to pursue his passion. One day, while browsing the shelves of an old bookstore in the nearby town, Liam stumbled upon a weathered book dedicated to snake farming. Intrigued, he purchased the book with the little money he had saved from odd jobs around the village. With the book in hand, Liam delved into its pages with unwavering determination. He read about snake behavior, habitat requirements, feeding habits, and even how to handle venomous species safely. Every spare moment he had was devoted to absorbing the knowledge within the book's well-worn covers. Equipped with the newfound knowledge, Liam decided to turn his passion into a purpose. He identified a small, unused plot of land on the outskirts of the village and began transforming it into a snake farm. He designed enclosures that mimicked natural habitats, carefully controlling temperature and humidity levels just as the book had instructed. Liam's first batch of snakes came from a nearby rescue center, where he adopted a variety of non-venomous species. He meticulously followed the guidelines from the book, ensuring that each snake received proper care and attention. Days turned into weeks, and Liam's dedication began to bear fruit. The snakes under his care thrived, and word of his successful snake farm spread through the village. As his reputation grew, so did Liam's ambition. He expanded his snake farm to include venomous species, implementing the safety protocols he had meticulously learned from the book. He even started collecting snake venom for medical research, partnering with local researchers to contribute to scientific advancements. Liam's snake farm became a thriving enterprise, attracting researchers, enthusiasts, and even tourists from neighboring regions. His success wasn't just financial; he had also become an advocate for snake conservation and education, using his farm as a platform to dispel myths and misconceptions about these remarkable creatures. Years passed, and Liam's snake farm flourished beyond his wildest dreams. He never forgot the role that book had played in his journey. In a corner of his office, he kept that weathered tome as a reminder of the power of knowledge and determination. The book that had once been his guide had transformed him from a curious village boy into a respected authority in the world of snake farming. And so, the story of Liam and his snake farm became an inspiring tale of how a single book, fueled by passion and fueled by knowledge, could lead to remarkable success and make a difference in both one person's life and the world around them.

In the realm where fascination meets practicality, lies the world of snake farming - a unique endeavor that marries the mystique of these slithering creatures with the principles of responsible husbandry. Whether you're a passionate reptile enthusiast or an aspiring entrepreneur seeking a niche in the animal husbandry domain, this guide is your passport to unlocking the captivating world of snake farming. Snake farming isn't merely a venture; it's a journey into the intricate lives of these creatures, an exploration of their diverse species, behaviors, and habitats, and a pursuit that demands both dedication and knowledge. In the pages that follow, we will embark on this journey together, delving into every aspect of snake farming – from the basics of setting up a farm to advanced breeding techniques, health care, and even ethical considerations. The aim of this guide is to equip you with the tools you need to start and sustain a successful snake farming enterprise. We'll navigate through the complexities of choosing the right snake species for your farm, creating suitable environments that mirror their natural habitats, and ensuring their wellbeing through proper nutrition and healthcare. Moreover, we'll delve into the nuances of snake breeding, including reproductive biology and hatchling care, as well as the responsible collection and handling of snake venom.But snake farming is more than a business venture; it's an opportunity to contribute to snake conservation, education, and public awareness. Throughout this guide, we'll emphasize the importance of ethical practices, conservation efforts, and the role that snake farming plays in both local economies and global biodiversity. Whether you're a novice seeking a comprehensive introduction or an experienced enthusiast looking to refine your techniques, this guide aims to cater to your needs. Alongside practical insights and step-by-step instructions, we'll share inspiring success stories, cautionary tales, and valuable tips from experts in the field. By the time you turn the final page, you'll possess a well-rounded understanding of snake farming – from its origins and challenges to its potential for innovation and positive impact. So, let's embark on this journey together – a journey that promises to unravel the secrets of snake farming and empower you to become a responsible, knowledgeable, and passionate guardian of these captivating creatures.

Chapter 1: Understanding the Relevance of Snake Farming

In the intricate tapestry of human interaction with the natural world, snake farming emerges as a compelling thread, weaving together conservation, science, public health, education, economics, ethics, and regulation. Within this multifaceted landscape, the relevance of snake farming unfurls in a panorama of interconnected domains, each deserving a careful and comprehensive exploration.

In the realm of conservation, snake farming assumes the mantle of a protector, safeguarding the delicate balance of biodiversity. It offers a lifeline to species teetering on the precipice of oblivion, providing a haven where controlled breeding mitigates the relentless onslaught of habitat loss and illegal trade. Snake farms transform into sanctuaries, nurturing endangered snakes to resurgence, their captive presence a glimmer of hope for the wild.

Embedded in the realm of scientific inquiry, snake farming unfetters the secrets of serpentine existence. Controlled environments become crucibles of understanding, enabling researchers to unravel intricate behavioral patterns, decode genetic enigmas, and probe venomous mysteries. The captive serpents become emissaries of knowledge, whispering tales of ecological interactions and unraveling the intricacies of life itself.

The practical marvels of snake farming extend to public health, where the potency of venom metamorphoses into a life-saving elixir. Snake venom, once a harbinger of peril, transforms into the cornerstone of antidote creation. Snake farms become repositories of antidotal promise, supplying the critical venom necessary for crafting antivenoms that combat the specter of snakebite fatalities.

An educational odyssey takes shape within the realm of snake farming, where myths and fears are exercised, and understanding blossoms. These sanctuaries of learning demystify serpents, fostering respect and coexistence. Snake farms metamorphose into immersive classrooms, nurturing generations versed in the art of harmonious interactions with these enigmatic creatures.

Venturing into the economic tapestry, snake farming pioneers a path toward sustainable livelihoods. Local communities find solace in the ethically balanced trade of snake-related products, from skins to traditional medicines. The economic symphony orchestrated by snake farming resonates through regions where these creatures, once feared, become agents of prosperity.

Yet, this tapestry is not devoid of ethical and regulatory considerations. The relevance of snake farming invokes introspection, demanding ethical breeding practices, responsible husbandry, and a harmony with ecological principles. A symphony of regulations orchestrates this industry, ensuring the harmonious coexistence of snakes, humanity, and the environment.

As the chapters of this exploration unfold, diverse voices resonate through case studies and interviews, illustrating the diverse perspectives that shape snake farming's narrative. Within this tapestry, the relevance of snake farming stands as a testament to humanity's capacity for stewardship, understanding, and innovation. It is a reflection of our endeavor to harmonize progress with nature, enriching the grand tapestry of existence.

Brief History of Snake Farming

Snake farming, also known as serpent farming, has a history rooted in various cultures and regions. It involves the controlled breeding and rearing of snakes for various purposes, including venom extraction, meat, leather, and even the pet trade. The origins of snake farming can be traced back to ancient civilizations such as the Egyptians and Greeks, who recognized the potential uses of snake venom for medicinal and religious purposes. In China, snake farming has historical roots in traditional medicine and cuisine. In the 20th century, snake farming gained traction for venom extraction, as snake venom were found to have valuable properties for producing antivenom and medical research. Snake farms began to emerge in different parts of the world, notably in Asia, Africa, and the Americas. Over time, snake farming evolved to include other purposes. In some regions, snake meat became a delicacy or a traditional dish, while snake leather found its place in the fashion industry. The exotic pet trade also fueled the demand for captive-bred snakes, leading to the establishment of snake farms that catered to this market.Snake farming has faced both criticism and support. Conservation concerns have been raised due to potential impacts on wild snake populations, especially if farm-bred snakes are released into the wild. However, responsible and well-regulated snake farming practices have also contributed to the protection of certain snake species by reducing the pressure on their natural habitats.In recent years, advancements in snake breeding techniques, veterinary care, and sustainable practices have further shaped the snake farming industry. The history of snake farming reflects the complex interplay between cultural traditions, economic opportunities, and conservation efforts.

Benefits and Challenges of Snake Farming

Snake farming, also known as serpentariums or snake breeding facilities, presents a unique blend of benefits and challenges that deserve careful consideration. Let's delve into the intriguing world of snake farming:

Benefits:

Conservation Efforts: Snake farming can contribute to the conservation of threatened or endangered snake species by providing a controlled environment for breeding and studying these creatures.

Anti-Venom Production: Venomous snake farming can serve as a vital resource for producing anti-venom, which is essential for treating snakebite victims. This helps save countless lives in regions where snakebites are prevalent.

Scientific Research: Snake farms provide researchers with a platform to study snake behavior, venom composition, and genetics, leading to a better understanding of these animals and potential medical applications.

Education and Awareness: Well-managed serpentariums offer educational opportunities for the public, fostering appreciation for snakes and dispelling myths and fears. This can lead to improved coexistence between humans and snakes.

Economic Revenue: Snake farming can generate income through tourism, the sale of snake-related products (such as skins, jewelry, and artifacts), and the export of snakes to pet markets.

Challenges:

Ethical Concerns: Keeping snakes in captivity raises ethical questions about their quality of life, especially for species with large ranges or specific habitat requirements.

Biosecurity Risks: Managing snake farms demands stringent biosecurity measures to prevent disease transmission between snakes and potential escape risks, which could harm local ecosystems.

Legal and Regulatory Hurdles: Many snake species are protected by laws and regulations, making it challenging to navigate the legal landscape of snake farming and trade.

Public Safety: The escape of venomous snakes poses significant public safety risks, particularly if they enter populated areas.

Environmental Impact: If not managed properly, snake farming could potentially lead to overexploitation of wild snake populations, disrupting ecosystems and biodiversity.

Stigma and Fear: Snake farming may face opposition due to deep-seated cultural fears and misunderstandings about these creatures, which can impact public perception and acceptance.

Chapter 2: Types of Snakes for Farming

Snake farming, also known as serpent farming or snake breeding, involves the controlled breeding and rearing of various species of snakes for a variety of purposes. While the practice may evoke images of danger and fear, snake farming serves multiple economic, ecological, and scientific roles. This chapter will delve into the different types of snake farming, their purposes, and potential benefits and concerns associated with each type.

1. **Venom Production:**

One of the most well-known purposes of snake farming is the extraction of venom for the production of antivenom, research, and pharmaceuticals. Venomous snake species such as cobras, vipers, and mambas are kept in controlled environments where skilled handlers extract their venom. This venom is then processed to create antivenom, which is used to treat snakebite victims. Snake farming for venom production not only saves lives but also contributes to scientific research into snake venoms and their potential medical applications.

2. Leather and Skins:

Certain non-venomous snake species are bred for their attractive and valuable skins. Snake leather is used in the fashion industry to create accessories, clothing, and luxury goods. Popular snake species for leather production include pythons, boas, and rat snakes. Sustainable and ethical snake farming practices can help reduce the demand for wild-caught snake skins, thus contributing to wildlife conservation efforts.

3. Pet Trade:

Many snake species are popular as exotic pets, and snake farming plays a role in meeting the demand for these reptiles. Breeding programs focus on producing captive-bred snakes, reducing the pressure on wild populations and helping to prevent illegal wildlife trafficking. Common pet snake species bred on farms include ball pythons, corn snakes, and king snakes.

4. Research and Education:

Snake farming can also serve as a valuable resource for scientific research and educational purposes. Breeding and studying different snake species in controlled environments can provide insights into their behavior, physiology, genetics, and ecological roles. These farms can also offer educational programs and demonstrations to promote understanding and appreciation of snakes, thereby dispelling myths and reducing fear.

5. Traditional Practices:

In some cultures, snakes hold religious, cultural, or medicinal significance. Snake farming may be carried out to fulfill traditional practices, such as snake handling in religious ceremonies or using snake byproducts in traditional medicine. These practices, however, can sometimes lead to ethical concerns and have potential conservation implications.

Benefits:

- Snake farming can reduce pressure on wild populations, aiding in wildlife conservation efforts.
- Controlled environments allow for the study of snake behavior, genetics, and venom, contributing to scientific knowledge.
- The production of antivenom from captive-bred snakes can save lives and improve medical treatments.
- Sustainable snake farming can support local economies, providing livelihoods and reducing poverty.

Concerns:
- Ethical considerations arise in cases where farming involves endangering wild populations or mistreatment of captive snakes.
- Disease management is crucial to prevent the spread of pathogens among captive snakes.
- Escapees from poorly managed farms can establish invasive populations and impact local ecosystems.
- The demand for certain snake products may perpetuate illegal wildlife trade if not properly regulated.

Venomous vs. Non-venomous Snakes: Understanding the key differences

Snakes, with their mesmerizing beauty and intriguing behaviors, have long captured the human imagination. However, they also evoke fear and caution due to the potential danger some species pose through their venomous bites. Distinguishing between venomous and non-venomous snakes is crucial for safety and appreciation of these remarkable creatures. In this chapter, we will delve into the characteristics, behaviors, and ecological roles of venomous and non-venomous snakes, highlighting their differences and dispelling common misconceptions.

1. **Anatomy and Venom Delivery:**

Venomous snakes possess specialized glands and fangs that produce and deliver venom into thoir prcy. These glands, located near the snake's upper jaw, secrete venom containing enzymes and toxins that immobilize or digest prey. In contrast, non-venomous snakes lack such adaptations and primarily rely on constriction or swallowing whole prey.

2. Fangs and Teeth:

Venomous snakes typically have hollow, retractable fangs designed for injecting venom. These fangs are located in the front of the mouth and fold up when the snake's mouth is closed. Non-venomous snakes possess solid teeth, which aid in capturing and manipulating their prey but lack the specialized delivery mechanism of venomous species.

3. Prey and Feeding Behavior:

Venomous snakes primarily hunt live prey, injecting venom to immobilize and initiate digestion before consumption. Non-venomous snakes employ a variety of feeding strategies, including constricting their prey to death, swallowing it whole, or using constriction in conjunction with venom to subdue their meals.

4. Defensive Behavior:

Venomous snakes may use their venom defensively if they feel threatened. They may strike or bite when provoked, injecting venom through their fangs. Non-venomous snakes, on the other hand, may bite if agitated, but their bites are generally harmless and serve as a means of defense rather than a venomous attack.

5. Venom Effects and Human Health:

Venomous snake bites can have serious health consequences for humans, ranging from mild symptoms to severe reactions that require medical attention. Envenomation can lead to tissue damage, bleeding, paralysis, or even death if left untreated. Non-venomous snakebites are usually harmless, causing minor injuries that may result in local swelling or irritation.

6. Ecological Roles:

Both venomous and non-venomous snakes play crucial roles in ecosystems. Non-venomous snakes help control rodent populations, maintaining ecological balance. Venomous snakes, despite their potentially harmful effects on humans, contribute to ecosystem health by controlling prey populations and influencing predator-prey dynamics.

7. Identification and Myths:

Proper identification of snake species is essential for safety. While some non-venomous snakes may resemble venomous ones, relying on myths or old wives' tales for identification is risky. Learning to identify key features such as head shape, pupil shape, and color patterns can aid in distinguishing between venomous and non-venomous snakes accurately.

Venomous and non-venomous snakes share the same order but differ significantly in their adaptations, behaviors, and effects on human health. Understanding these differences fosters a deeper appreciation for these creatures and promotes responsible coexistence. Remember, when encountering any snake in the wild, it's best to observe from a safe distance and avoid provoking or handling them to ensure both your safety and the snake's well-being.

Exploring Popular Snake Species for Farming: A Comprehensive Overview

Snake farming, also known as serpent farming or snake ranching, has gained attention in recent years as a unique and potentially profitable agricultural endeavor. While the practice presents its challenges and requires careful management, it offers opportunities for venom extraction, pet trade, and even conservation efforts. In this comprehensive guide, we will delve into some of the popular snake species that are commonly farmed and highlight key considerations for successful snake farming operations.

1. **Ball Python (Python regius):**

Ball pythons are renowned for their docile nature, relatively manageable size, and captivating color variations. They are highly sought after in the pet trade due to their attractive appearance and ease of care. Snake farmers often breed ball pythons for their vibrant morphs, which can fetch premium prices from enthusiasts.

2. Corn Snake (Pantherophis guttatus):

Corn snakes are another popular choice among snake farmers. Their appealing patterns, adaptability, and relatively small size make them ideal candidates for captive breeding. Corn snakes come in a wide range of colors and patterns, making them a favorite among both novice and experienced snake enthusiasts.

3. Boa Constrictor (Boa constrictor):

Boa constrictors are larger snakes that can be challenging to manage, but their impressive size and docile temperament make them appealing for snake farming. They are also bred for their morphs, which can result in striking variations in color and pattern.

4. King Cobra (Ophiophagus hannah):

While more challenging to farm due to their venomous nature, some snake farms work with king cobras for their potent venom. Venom extraction from king cobras has potential pharmaceutical applications, and captive breeding could help reduce pressure on wild populations.

5. Green Tree Python (Morelia viridis):

Known for their stunning emerald green coloration and arboreal habits, green tree pythons are a favorite among advanced snake keepers and breeders. They require specialized care, including vertical enclosures and high humidity levels, making them a niche species for dedicated snake farms.

6. Garter Snake (Thamnophis spp.):

Garter snakes are smaller, non-venomous species that are often chosen for their ease of care and reproductive capabilities. They are often used in educational programs and can be bred for educational purposes or the pet trade.

7. Rat Snake (Elaphe spp.):

Rat snakes are known for their rat-hunting abilities and come in various species and subspecies. They are valued for their role in controlling rodent populations. Snake farmers may choose rat snakes for their hardiness and relatively straightforward husbandry requirements.

Key Considerations for Snake Farming:

1. **Legal and Ethical Considerations:** Check local and international laws regarding snake farming, permits, and trade. Ensure ethical practices, including responsible breeding and animal welfare.

2. **Enclosure Design:** Different snake species have varied habitat requirements. Design and maintain enclosures that mimic their natural environment, including temperature, humidity, and hiding spots.

3. **Breeding Programs:** Establish successful breeding programs to ensure healthy captive

populations. Consider factors like mating compatibility, incubation conditions, and neonate care.

4. **Health and Nutrition:** Maintain optimal health by providing proper nutrition and regular veterinary care. Monitor for signs of illness and handle snakes with care to minimize stress.

5. **Market Research:** Understand the demand and trends in the pet trade or pharmaceutical industry for specific snake species or their products, such as venom.

6. **Education and Outreach:** Use snake farming as an opportunity for conservation education, dispelling myths, and promoting responsible snake ownership.

In conclusion, snake farming can offer both financial opportunities and conservation benefits. However, it requires dedication, knowledge, and adherence to legal and ethical standards. By selecting appropriate snake species and implementing proper husbandry practices, snake farmers can contribute to conservation, research, and the thriving pet trade industry while respecting the welfare of these fascinating reptiles.

Considerations for Snake Selection

Selecting the right snake species for a snake farm is a critical decision that directly impacts the success and sustainability of your operation. Below is a comprehensive guide to help you make informed choices:

1. **Market Research:** Conduct thorough market research to identify demand and trends for various snake species. Consider factors like pet trade, venom extraction, and educational programs to determine which snakes are in demand and can generate revenue for your snake farm.

2. **Local Regulations:** Familiarize yourself with local, regional, and national regulations governing

the ownership, breeding, and trade of snake species. Ensure that the species you choose can be legally kept and traded in your area.

3. **Species Selection:** Choose snake species that are well-suited to captivity, have a manageable temperament, and can thrive in your climate. Consider factors such as size, feeding habits, reproductive potential, and adaptability to captive conditions.

4. **Habitat Requirements:** Research the specific habitat needs of each chosen snake species. Design enclosures that closely mimic their natural environment, including temperature, humidity, lighting, and substrate.

5. **Feeding and Nutrition:** Understand the dietary preferences and requirements of the selected snakes. Ensure a reliable and sustainable source of food, whether it's live prey, pre-killed rodents, or other appropriate options.

6. **Health Considerations:** Prioritize the health and well-being of your snakes. Regularly monitor their condition, provide proper veterinary care, and quarantine new arrivals to prevent the spread of diseases.

7. **Breeding Potential:** If breeding is a goal, select snake species with documented breeding success in captivity. Consider factors such as gestation period, litter size, and ease of reproduction.

8. **Genetic Diversity:** Maintain genetic diversity within your snake population to prevent inbreeding and associated health issues. Plan breeding programs that prioritize genetic variability.

9. **Expertise and Training:** Ensure that you and your staff have the necessary expertise and training to handle and care for the selected snake species. Proper handling techniques, venom extraction (if applicable), and overall snake husbandry are crucial skills.

10. **Safety Measures:** Implement strict safety protocols to prevent escapes and ensure the safety of your staff and visitors. Venomous species, if present, require specialized handling and safety measures.

11. **Education and Outreach:** Consider the educational potential of the snake species you choose. Some snakes may be suitable for educational programs, public demonstrations, and outreach activities, enhancing your farm's visibility and impact.

12. **Sustainability:** Prioritize sustainable practices to minimize the impact on wild populations. Avoid harvesting snakes from the wild and explore captive breeding programs to meet demand.

Chapter 3: Setting Up a Snake Farm

Setting up a snake farm is a multifaceted and intricate venture that demands meticulous planning, in-depth research, and a profound commitment to the welfare of both the snakes and the personnel involved. This chapter will walk you through the intricate process of establishing a snake farm, covering all the crucial aspects and considerations.

1. **Research and Planning:** Embark on an exhaustive research journey to comprehend the diverse range of snake species you intend to house. Grasp their specific habitat requisites, behavioral patterns, dietary preferences, and distinct health demands. Establish a clear purpose for your snake farm, be it for conservation efforts, educational purposes, or commercial breeding.

2. **Legal Considerations:** Familiarize yourself with the myriad of local, regional, and national

regulations pertaining to snake ownership, breeding, and public exhibition. Prioritize acquiring the necessary permits and licenses before embarking on any further steps.

3. **Location and Infrastructure:** Deliberate on the ideal location for your snake farm, taking into account factors like accessibility, security, and the availability of essential utilities. Construct meticulously designed enclosures that cater to the particular needs of each snake species. Ensure that enclosures encompass suitable dimensions, appropriate substrates, and furnishings that simulate the snakes' natural habitats.

4. **Quarantine and Health Measures:** Institute a stringent quarantine protocol for newly acquired snakes to mitigate the potential spread of diseases. Develop a robust health monitoring regimen and establish a collaborative partnership with a veterinarian who possesses substantial experience in reptile health.

5. **Snake Acquisition:** Source your snake specimens from reputable breeders, established institutions, or responsible collectors. Embrace ethical practices by refraining from capturing snakes from the wild, as this can contribute to ecological imbalances and declining snake populations.

6. **Feeding and Nutrition:** Formulate a meticulously balanced diet tailored to the distinct requirements of each snake species. Factors such as size, age, and dietary preferences should be weighed in. Ensure a consistent and reliable supply of appropriate prey items and observe feeding habits attentively.

7. **Environmental Enrichment:** Devise an environment that nurtures the manifestation of natural behaviors among your snakes. Craft enclosures that incorporate various elements such as hiding spots, climbing opportunities, and basking locales. These enrichment activities are pivotal in enhancing the mental and physical well-being of the snakes.

8. **Breeding Programs: a**lf your snake farm embraces breeding initiatives, delve into the specialized breeding requirements for each distinct species. Construct adequate nesting sites, establish controlled temperature fluctuations, and manipulate photoperiods to stimulate the reproductive process.

9. **Visitor Experience and Education:** Should you choose to open your snake farm to the public, create captivating and educational displays that disseminate knowledge about snakes, their ecological significance, and ongoing conservation endeavors. Develop engaging guided tours to foster awareness and understanding.

10. **Staff Training:** Prioritize comprehensive training for your staff members in the domains of snake handling, adherence to safety protocols, and effective execution of emergency procedures. By ensuring that your staff is well-prepared, you minimize risks and uphold the safety of both the personnel and the snakes.

11 **Health and Safety Protocols:** Forge stringent safety protocols that dictate the proper handling of venomous snakes. Enforce the utilization of appropriate personal protective equipment (PPE) and elucidate comprehensive first aid measures. Establish a well-equipped medical facility on-site to cater to any unforeseen emergencies.

12. **Record Keeping:** Imperative to the smooth functioning of your snake farm is the diligent maintenance of meticulous records for each individual snake. These records should encompass acquisition dates, comprehensive health assessments, feeding schedules, and any breeding activities. The precision of these records is instrumental in efficient monitoring and management.

13. **Networking and Collaboration:** Nurture a network of connections with other snake farms, conservation organizations, and herpetological

Choosing the Right Location

Selecting the optimal location for setting up a snake farm is a pivotal decision that profoundly impacts the success and sustainability of your venture. Careful consideration of various factors is crucial to ensure that the chosen site caters to the unique requirements of housing and managing snake species. Here's a comprehensive overview of the key considerations when choosing the right location for your snake farm:

1. **Accessibility:** Choose a location that is easily accessible for both staff and potential visitors. Proximity to major transportation routes, airports, and urban centers will facilitate the transportation of snakes, supplies, and the arrival of guests.

2. **Climate and Geography:** Evaluate the climate of the chosen area and determine whether it aligns with the climatic needs of the snake species you intend to house. Certain snake species require specific

temperature and humidity ranges. Additionally, consider the geographical features of the site, such as elevation, terrain, and soil composition, which can affect enclosure design and construction.

3. **Security and Safety:** Prioritize security by selecting a site with low crime rates and a stable socio-political environment. Ensure that the chosen location adheres to local safety codes and regulations. Implement robust security measures to prevent theft, vandalism, or unauthorized access to the snake farm.

4. **Zoning and Permits:** Thoroughly research local zoning regulations and land-use policies to confirm that a snake farm is permissible in the chosen area. Obtain all necessary permits and licenses from local authorities before proceeding with any construction or operation.

5. **Utilities and Infrastructure:** Check the availability of essential utilities such as water, electricity, and gas. A reliable power supply is crucial to maintaining appropriate lighting, heating, and

ventilation within snake enclosures. Adequate infrastructure, including roads and utilities, will facilitate smooth operations.

6. **Environmental Impact:** Assess the potential environmental impact of your snake farm on the surrounding ecosystem. Take measures to minimize any negative effects, especially if you plan to release snakes into the wild as part of a conservation effort.

7. **Space and Expansion:** Choose a site that offers ample space for current and future needs. Consider the possibility of expanding enclosures, building educational facilities, or establishing research laboratories. Adequate space allows for the growth and diversification of your snake farm's activities.

8. **Local Community:** Engage with the local community and gauge their sentiment towards your snake farm project. Building positive relationships with neighbors can mitigate potential conflicts and foster community support.

9. **Noise and Visual Impact:** Evaluate the potential noise and visual impact of the snake farm on the surrounding area. Implement measures to minimize noise disruptions and ensure that the farm's appearance is aesthetically pleasing and in harmony with the environment.

10. **Natural Resources:** Conduct a thorough assessment of available natural resources, such as water sources, flora, and fauna. Implement sustainable practices to minimize resource consumption and support local biodiversity.

11. **Market Access:** Consider the proximity of your snake farm to potential markets for snake-related products or services. If you plan to sell snakes, venom, or related products, being strategically located can enhance your business prospects.

12. **Employee Availability:** Evaluate the availability of skilled personnel in the chosen location. Consider factors such as the local labor market, education institutions offering relevant programs, and the potential to attract qualified staff.

Designing Snake Enclosures for a Thriving Snake Farm: Balancing Welfare and Efficiency

At the heart of a successful snake farm lies the art and science of designing optimal snake enclosures. These enclosures serve as the living spaces for a diverse array of snake species, each with unique requirements and behaviors. Creating a snake enclosure system that prioritizes the well-being of the snakes while maximizing efficiency is a critical aspect of running a successful snake farm. In this guide, we will explore the key factors to consider when designing snake enclosures for a snake farm.

1. **Comprehensive Research and Planning:** Before embarking on the design process, thorough research is paramount. Understand the specific needs of each snake species that will inhabit the farm. Factors such as temperature ranges, humidity levels, substrate preferences, and natural behaviors

must be carefully considered to ensure that the enclosures closely mimic the snakes' native habitats.

2. **Enclosure Variety and Flexibility:** A diverse range of enclosures is essential to accommodate the various snake species at your farm. From arboreal setups for tree-dwelling species to spacious terrestrial enclosures for ground-dwellers, providing a variety of enclosure types ensures that each snake's needs are met. Additionally, designing enclosures that allow for easy modification and customization will enable you to adapt to new species or changing requirements.

3. **Space Optimization and Efficiency:** Efficient space utilization is key to a productive snake farm. Consider the layout of enclosures, pathways, and work areas to maximize both snake welfare and staff productivity. Utilize vertical space for arboreal species and implement a system that minimizes wasted space while providing adequate room for each snake.

4. **Climate Control and Monitoring:** Maintaining consistent and appropriate environmental conditions is crucial for snake health. Implement a robust climate control system that includes temperature regulation, humidity management, and adequate ventilation. Incorporate monitoring systems to ensure that conditions remain within the desired range at all times.

5. **Hygiene and Sanitation:** A clean and hygienic environment is essential for preventing the spread of diseases and maintaining snake health. Design enclosures with easy-to-clean surfaces and materials. Develop a comprehensive cleaning and sanitation protocol to ensure enclosures are regularly maintained.

6. **Safety Measures:** Safety considerations are paramount on a snake farm. Design enclosures with secure locks and mechanisms to prevent escapes and unauthorized access. Ensure that enclosures are escape-proof and resistant to external threats.

7. **Feeding and Enrichment:** Incorporate feeding stations that allow for efficient and stress-free feeding of the snakes. Enrichment items, such as climbing structures, hiding spots, and objects that encourage natural behaviors, should be strategically placed within enclosures to promote mental and physical stimulation.

8. **Quarantine and Isolation Facilities:** Designate a separate area for quarantine and isolation enclosures to prevent the spread of diseases and parasites. Implement strict protocols for introducing new snakes to the farm and monitor their health before integrating them into the main facility.

9. **Educational Displays:** A well-designed snake farm can also serve as an educational hub for visitors. Consider creating informative displays that showcase different snake species, their habitats, and conservation efforts. Incorporating educational signage and interactive elements can enhance the visitor experience and promote awareness about snakes and their importance in ecosystems.

10. **Continuous Evaluation and Improvement:** The design of snake enclosures should be an ongoing process. Regularly assess the functionality of enclosures, gather feedback from staff, and make adjustments as needed to ensure that the snakes are thriving and the farm operations are running smoothly.

In conclusion, designing snake enclosures for a snake farm requires a harmonious blend of animal welfare, efficiency, and functionality. By meticulously considering the needs of the snake species, implementing state-of-the-art climate control systems, prioritizing hygiene, and embracing flexibility, you can create a thriving snake farm that provides a safe, stimulating, and educational environment for both the snakes and those who visit the farm.

Mastering the Art of Temperature and Humidity Control: Vital Principles for a Thriving Snake Farm

As stewards of these magnificent creatures, it is our responsibility to create an environment that mirrors their natural habitats and ensures their well-being. In this comprehensive guide, we will delve into the crucial principles and best practices for achieving optimal temperature and humidity levels on your snake farm.

Understanding the Dynamics:

1. **Temperature:** Snakes are ectothermic creatures, meaning their body temperature is influenced by their environment. A well-regulated temperature range is vital for their physiological processes, digestion, and overall health. From basking spots that mimic sunlight to cooler retreats for

thermoregulation, providing a temperature gradient within enclosures ensures snakes can move to their preferred comfort zone.

2. **Humidity:** Humidity levels play a pivotal role in maintaining proper shedding cycles and respiratory health. Different snake species have varying humidity requirements, mirroring their natural habitats. Striking the right balance between ambient humidity and targeted humid hides fosters healthy skin shedding and prevents dehydration.

Best Practices for Temperature Control:

1. **Heat Sources:** Incorporate heat sources such as under-tank heaters, heat mats, ceramic heat emitters, or radiant heat panels. These options provide a gentle warmth, simulating natural sun exposure, and should be controlled by thermostats to prevent overheating.

2. **Thermal Gradients:** Design enclosures with temperature gradients, allowing snakes to move between warmer and cooler areas. Utilize temperature-regulating elements like heat rocks or heated perches for basking, combined with cooler hide boxes for retreat.

Mastering Humidity Management:

1. **Humidity Boxes:** Introduce humidity hides or boxes filled with damp substrate to create localized high humidity zones. This is especially crucial during shedding periods to facilitate successful skin shedding.

2. **Substrate Selection:** Choose substrates that retain moisture, such as coconut coir, sphagnum moss, or cypress mulch. Regularly misting

enclosures or incorporating automated misting systems can help maintain humidity levels.

Advanced Techniques:

1. **Automated Systems:** Employ advanced technology like humidity controllers and misting systems to regulate humidity levels with precision. These systems offer hands-free maintenance and ensure consistent conditions.

2. **Environmental Monitoring:** Install temperature and humidity monitors to continually assess the enclosure environment. Real-time data helps identify fluctuations and enables prompt adjustments.

Fine-Tuning for Success:

1. **Species-Specific Care:** Tailor temperature and humidity control to the specific needs of each snake

species on your farm. Extensive research and observation are essential to emulate their native habitats accurately.

2. **Regular Assessment:** Continuously monitor and adjust temperature and humidity levels based on seasonal changes and individual snake behavior. Record-keeping aids in identifying patterns and optimizing conditions.

Ensuring Safety on the Snake Farm: Essential Measures for Responsible Snake Handling

Safety is paramount in every facet of our snake farming endeavors. As we work passionately to care for and study these remarkable creatures, it is imperative that we prioritize the well-being of both our staff and the snakes themselves. In this comprehensive guide, we will explore the critical safety measures that must be adhered to on our snake farm to ensure a secure and productive environment.

1. **Training and Education:**

- **Comprehensive Training:** All staff members must undergo thorough training in snake behavior, handling techniques, and emergency procedures before interacting with the snakes.

- **Continuous Learning:** Stay updated on the latest research and best practices in snake handling through workshops, seminars, and ongoing education.

2. **Personal Protective Equipment (PPE):**

- **Proper Attire:** Wear appropriate clothing that covers the skin to prevent potential bites or scratches. Gloves specifically designed for snake handling can offer added protection.

- Eye Protection: Wear safety glasses or goggles to safeguard your eyes from potential snake strikes.

3. Handling Procedures:

- Two-Person Rule: Whenever possible, snake handling should involve at least two trained personnel to ensure effective control and response.

- Calm and Gentle Approach: Handle snakes with slow, deliberate movements to avoid startling or stressing them. Minimize sudden or abrupt actions.

- Avoid Agitation: Recognize signs of stress in snakes, such as hissing or defensive postures. Handle them only when necessary, and with caution.

4. Proper Equipment:

- Snake Hooks and Tongs: Utilize snake hooks or tongs for initial handling and movement of snakes. These tools allow for a safe distance between the handler and the snake.

- Snake Bags or Tubes: When necessary, use specialized bags or tubes for more secure containment during tasks like cleaning enclosures or veterinary procedures.

5. **Enclosure Design:**

- **Escape-Proof Enclosures:** Design snake enclosures with secure locks and mechanisms to prevent escapes. Regularly inspect enclosures for any potential vulnerabilities.

- **Accessibility:** Ensure that enclosures are designed to allow for safe and efficient access during cleaning, feeding, and other tasks.

6. **First Aid and Emergency Response:**

- **Well-Stocked First Aid Kits:** Keep fully equipped first aid kits on-site, including materials for snake bite treatment, wound care, and emergency medical supplies.

- **Emergency Protocols:** Establish clear protocols for responding to snake-related incidents, including snake escapes, bites, and medical emergencies.

7. **Health and Hygiene:**

- **Personal Hygiene:** Wash hands thoroughly after handling snakes or working in snake enclosures to prevent potential transmission of pathogens.

- **Quarantine Measures:** Implement a rigorous quarantine process for new snakes entoring the farm to prevent the introduction of diseases.

8. **Visitor Safety:**

- **Educational Outreach:** Educate visitors about safe snake interactions and the importance of following guidelines.
- **Controlled Interactions:** If allowing public interactions with snakes, provide supervised, controlled environments with trained handlers.

By adhering to these safety measures and fostering a culture of responsibility, we can ensure the well-being of both our team members and the snakes under our care. Let us remain steadfast in our commitment to safe practices as we continue our important work on our snake farm.

Chapter 4: Feeding and Nutrition on a Snake Farm

Maintaining the health and well-being of snakes on a farm is a crucial aspect of responsible reptile husbandry. Proper feeding and nutrition play a pivotal role in ensuring the snakes' growth, vitality, and overall health. A snake farm is a controlled environment where various species of snakes are bred, kept, and sometimes even raised for different purposes, such as scientific research, pet trade, or venom production. Here's a comprehensive guide to feeding and nutrition practices on a snake farm:

1. **Understanding Snake Diets:** Snakes are carnivorous reptiles, primarily feeding on live or pre-killed prey. The specific diet of a snake species depends on its natural habitat, size, and dietary preferences. Common snake prey includes rodents (mice, rats), birds, amphibians, and other small mammals. The nutritional requirements of snakes differ throughout their life stages, from hatchlings to adults.

2. **Selecting Proper Prey:** Snake farm operators must choose prey items that match the size and dietary preferences of each snake species. Offering a variety of prey species ensures a balanced diet and prevents nutritional deficiencies. Frozen-thawed prey is often preferred, as it eliminates the risk of injury to snakes during feeding and minimizes the transmission of diseases that live prey might carry.

3. **Feeding Schedule:** Establishing a consistent feeding schedule is essential for maintaining the health of snakes. Younger snakes may require more frequent feedings, while adults can be fed less frequently. Snakes can be fed every 5-14 days,

depending on their species and age. Monitoring the snakes' body condition and behavior helps adjust the feeding schedule accordingly.

4. **Monitoring Body Condition:** Regularly assessing the body condition of snakes is vital. An underweight snake may indicate insufficient feeding, while an overweight snake may need to be fed less frequently. A healthy snake should display a proportionate body shape and clear muscle definition.

5. **Providing Water:** Clean and accessible water should always be available for the snakes. Proper hydration is essential for digestion, shedding, and overall health. Snake farm operators must ensure water bowls are appropriately sized and placed to prevent accidental soaking or spillage.

6. **Nutritional Supplements:** In some cases, snake farm operators might need to provide nutritional supplements to ensure snakes receive all essential nutrients. Calcium and vitamin supplements may be dusted onto prey items before feeding to prevent

metabolic bone disease and other nutritional deficiencies.

7. **Feeding Techniques:** Different snake species may require various feeding techniques. For instance, some snakes prefer to hunt in an ambush style, while others may actively search for prey. Providing a suitable environment that mimics the snake's natural hunting behavior can enhance feeding success.

8. **Record Keeping:** Maintaining detailed records of each snake's feeding history, shedding cycles, and overall health is crucial. This information helps track their growth, detect potential health issues, and adjust feeding routines as needed.

9. **Health Monitoring:** Regular veterinary check-ups and health assessments are essential to identify and address any underlying health concerns. Snake farm operators should establish a working relationship with a reptile veterinarian who can provide expert advice and care.

10. **Ethical Considerations:** Snake farming should always prioritize the welfare of the animals. Overfeeding, inadequate prey size, and neglecting nutritional needs can lead to health problems. Adhering to ethical guidelines ensures the well-being of the snakes and upholds the reputation of the snake farming industry.

Proper feeding and nutrition practices are fundamental to the success of a snake farm. By understanding the dietary requirements of various snake species, providing appropriate prey items, maintaining a consistent feeding schedule, and monitoring the snakes' health, operators can ensure the well-being of their snake population and contribute to the responsible management of these fascinating reptiles.

Prey Selection and Preparation for Snakes on a Snake Farm:

Proper prey selection and preparation are crucial components of snake husbandry on a snake farm. Ensuring that the snakes receive a balanced and nutritious diet is essential for their overall health and well-being. In this comprehensive guide, we will delve into the intricate aspects of prey selection, preparation, and feeding techniques to provide the best care for snakes in a controlled environment.

1. **Prey Selection:**
Choosing the right prey items is a fundamental aspect of snake care. Prey selection should take into account the snake species, size, age, and natural diet in the wild. Snakes are carnivorous and consume a variety of prey, including rodents, birds, and amphibians. Researching the specific dietary

preferences of the snake species in question is crucial for meeting their nutritional needs.

2. Nutritional Requirements:

Prey items should be nutritionally balanced to provide snakes with the necessary proteins, fats, vitamins, and minerals. Nutrient content varies among prey species, so offering a diverse diet helps prevent nutritional deficiencies. Variety also stimulates natural feeding behaviors and promotes better digestion. Consulting with a veterinarian or reptile nutrition expert can help create a well-rounded diet plan.

3. Prey Size and Frequency:

Selecting the appropriate prey size is essential to prevent feeding-related issues. The prey size should be proportionate to the snake's size, allowing it to swallow the prey comfortably. Young snakes typically require smaller prey items and more frequent feedings compared to adults. The frequency of feedings should be tailored to the snake's age, species, and individual metabolism.

4. Prey Preparation:

Preparation methods depend on whether live, pre-killed, or frozen-thawed prey is used. Live prey carries risks, including injury to the snake or refusal to eat. Pre-killed and frozen-thawed prey are safer alternatives. To prepare frozen-thawed prey, follow these steps:

a. Thaw the prey item in a refrigerator overnight or using warm water.

b. Warm the prey to slightly above room temperature before feeding.

c. Use tongs to offer the prey to the snake, mimicking natural movement.

5. Feeding Techniques:

Feeding techniques vary based on the snake's behavior and feeding response. Some snakes readily accept pre-killed or frozen-thawed prey, while others may require live prey to stimulate their hunting instincts. However, feeding live prey can pose risks to both the snake and the keeper, and caution is necessary to ensure safety.

6. Monitoring and Adjustments:

Regularly monitor the snake's feeding response, body condition, and overall health. Adjust prey size and feeding frequency if needed. An underfed snake may exhibit reduced energy and weight loss, while an overfed snake could become obese. Consistent observation helps maintain a healthy weight and optimal body condition.

7. Ethical Considerations:

Ethical considerations play a significant role in prey selection. Whenever possible, opt for captive-bred prey items to reduce the impact on wild populations. Sustainable sourcing of both snakes and prey contributes to conservation efforts and responsible snake farming practices.

8. Record Keeping:

Maintaining accurate records of each snake's feeding history is essential for tracking their dietary needs and preferences. Record the date of feeding, prey type and size, and any observations regarding the snake's response to the meal.

9. **Continuous Learning**:

Staying informed about the latest advancements in snake nutrition and husbandry practices is essential for providing the best care. Attend workshops, seminars, and engage with fellow snake farm keepers to exchange knowledge and experiences.

In conclusion, prey selection and preparation are critical aspects of snake farming that directly impact the health and well-being of the snakes in your care. A thorough understanding of the snake species, their natural diet, and proper feeding techniques ensures that the snakes receive a balanced and nutritious diet. By prioritizing ethical sourcing and staying informed about best practices, snake farm keepers contribute to the conservation and responsible management of these remarkable reptiles.

Feeding Schedule and Portion Control

Maintaining a proper feeding schedule and practicing effective portion control is paramount for the well-being and health of the snake inhabitants on a snake farm. Snakes are ectothermic creatures, relying on external heat sources to regulate their body temperature. As such, their metabolism and feeding habits differ from those of endothermic animals. Establishing a well-structured feeding regimen and managing portion sizes are essential components of snake husbandry.

1. **Feeding Schedule:**

Creating a consistent feeding schedule is crucial to mimic natural feeding patterns and maintain the snakes' health. Factors such as species, age, size, and reproductive status play a significant role in determining the appropriate feeding frequency. Typically, younger snakes require more frequent meals to support growth, while adult snakes may have less frequent feeding intervals.

2. **Portion Control:**

Determining the right portion size for each snake is essential to prevent overfeeding or underfeeding. Offering prey items that are appropriately sized relative to the snake's girth ensures efficient digestion and minimizes the risk of regurgitation. Portion control also helps prevent obesity, a common issue among captive snakes, which can lead to various health problems.

3. **Prey Selection:**

Choosing appropriate prey items is essential for the snake's nutritional needs. Prey items should match the snake's natural diet and size, ensuring a balanced nutritional intake. It's important to offer a variety of prey items to provide essential nutrients and avoid nutritional deficiencies.

4. **Handling and Observation:**

Feeding time is also an opportunity to closely observe the snakes for any signs of illness or abnormalities. Regular handling during feeding can help habituate the snakes to human interaction and reduce stress during routine health checks.

5. **Adjusting Feeding Schedule:**

The feeding schedule should be adjusted based on factors such as shedding, reproductive cycle, and overall health. Snakes often reduce their appetite before shedding, and pregnant or breeding females may have different nutritional requirements.

6. **Hydration and Resting Periods:**

Incorporating regular hydration periods and fasting days into the feeding schedule can promote healthy digestion and metabolic processes. Snakes in the wild often experience periods of reduced feeding due to environmental factors, so replicating these cycles in captivity can contribute to the overall well-being of the animals.

7. **Veterinary Guidance:**

Regular consultations with a veterinarian experienced in reptile care are essential to ensure that the feeding schedule and portion control align with the specific needs of the snake species. A veterinarian can provide guidance on appropriate prey items, portion sizes, and any necessary supplements.

In conclusion, maintaining a well-structured feeding schedule and practicing effective portion control are fundamental aspects of snake farm management. By closely mimicking natural feeding patterns, providing appropriately sized prey items, and making adjustments based on the snakes' needs, snake farm owners can ensure the health, longevity, and overall well-being of their reptile residents. Regular observation, veterinary consultations, and a thorough understanding of each species' requirements are key to successful snake husbandry.

Chapter 5: Breeding and Reproduction of Snakes

Breeding snakes on a snake farm is a fascinating and intricate process that requires careful planning, knowledge of the species' reproductive biology, and meticulous attention to environmental conditions. Successful snake breeding contributes to genetic diversity, conservation efforts, and the overall sustainability of captive snake populations. Here's a comprehensive overview of the breeding and reproduction process on a snake farm:

1. **Species Selection and Compatibility:** Choosing suitable snake species for breeding is the first step. Knowledge of each species' reproductive behavior, seasonal patterns, and compatibility is crucial. Some snake species require specific environmental conditions or stimuli to initiate breeding behaviors.

2. **Preparation and Conditioning:** Prior to breeding, snakes may undergo a period of

conditioning. This includes ensuring proper nutrition, maintaining appropriate temperature and humidity levels, and creating a comfortable and secure habitat. Adequate conditioning helps enhance the snakes' reproductive health and increases the likelihood of successful breeding.

3. **Seasonal Cues and Breeding Behavior:** Many snake species are influenced by seasonal changes in temperature and daylight duration. These cues trigger breeding behaviors such as courtship, mating, and ovulation. Creating simulated seasonal cycles through controlled lighting and temperature adjustments can stimulate these behaviors in captive snakes.

4. **Courtship and Mating:** Courtship rituals and behaviors vary between snake species. Males may engage in elaborate displays, body movements, and pheromone releases to attract females. Once courtship is successful, mating occurs. Proper supervision during this phase is important to prevent aggressive interactions or potential harm to the snakes.

5. **Gestation and Oviposition:** Depending on the species, gestation periods can vary from weeks to months. Some snakes give birth to live young (viviparous), while others lay eggs (oviparous). Creating suitable nesting or egg-laying environments is crucial for the snakes' reproductive success. Providing proper substrate and humidity levels ensures the eggs or neonates develop appropriately.

6. **Incubation and Hatchling Care:** For egg-laying species, incubating the eggs at specific temperatures and humidity levels is essential for successful hatching. Careful monitoring during this phase helps prevent complications and ensures healthy hatchlings. Once the eggs hatch, neonates may require specific care, including feeding and habitat adjustments.

7. **Health and Genetic Considerations:** Regular health checks and genetic diversity assessments are vital to maintaining the overall well-being of the snake population. Inbreeding and genetic anomalies

can lead to health issues, so managing breeding pairs and tracking lineage is crucial.

8. **Record Keeping and Documentation:** Detailed record keeping of breeding cycles, behaviors, and outcomes is essential for snake farm management. This documentation helps track breeding success, lineage, and genetic information, facilitating informed decision-making for future breeding efforts.

9. **Conservation and Research:** Breeding programs on snake farms contribute to conservation efforts by preserving and protecting rare or endangered snake species. Additionally, snake farms provide opportunities for research into reproductive biology, behavior, and genetics, furthering our understanding of these enigmatic creatures.

Breeding and reproduction of snakes on a snake farm is a complex process that requires a deep understanding of each species' biology and behaviors. By providing suitable conditions, monitoring reproductive cycles, and practicing responsible breeding techniques, snake farm owners can contribute to the preservation of snake species, genetic diversity, and scientific knowledge, all while ensuring the well-being of their captive snake populations.

Snake Reproductive Biology on a Snake Farm

Understanding the reproductive biology of snakes is essential for successful breeding and conservation efforts on a snake farm. Snake reproductive processes are diverse and intriguing, encompassing various strategies and adaptations that have evolved over millions of years. Here is a comprehensive overview of snake reproductive biology as it pertains to a snake farm:

1. **Sexual Dimorphism:** Many snake species exhibit sexual dimorphism, where males and females have distinct physical differences. These differences can include variations in size, coloration, or scale patterns. Recognizing sexual dimorphism is crucial

for accurately identifying and pairing breeding individuals

2. **Reproductive Anatomy:** Snakes possess internal reproductive structures, including paired ovaries in females and hemipenes (paired copulatory organs) in males. The mating process involves the insertion of hemipenes into the female's cloaca, allowing for sperm transfer.

3. **Oviparous and Viviparous Species:** Snake species are categorized as oviparous (egg-laying) or viviparous (live-bearing). Oviparous snakes lay eggs that develop externally, while viviparous species give birth to live young after embryos develop internally. Snake farm operators must be familiar with the reproductive strategies of their target species.

4. **Egg Development and Laying:** Oviparous snakes produce eggs that are fertilized internally before being laid. The eggs are surrounded by a protective membrane, and their development is influenced by temperature and humidity. Snake farm

staff must create suitable nesting environments to support successful egg incubation.

5. **Viviparity and Placentation:** Viviparous snakes nourish embryos internally through placenta connections. Embryos receive nutrients and oxygen from the mother's bloodstream via specialized structures. Proper care and monitoring of pregnant viviparous snakes are essential to ensure successful gestation and parturition.

6. **Courtship and Mating:** Courtship behaviors vary widely among snake species. Males may engage in intricate courtship rituals involving body movements, displays, and pheromone release. Successful courtship leads to copulation, during which sperm transfer occurs.

7. **Gestation Periods:** The duration of gestation varies significantly between species. It can range from a few weeks to several months, depending on factors such as temperature, nutrition, and genetics. Understanding the specific gestation requirements

of each species is crucial for effective breeding management

8. **Egg Incubation:** For egg-laying species, creating optimal incubation conditions is vital for successful hatching. Temperature and humidity levels must be carefully controlled to ensure proper embryo development. Regular monitoring of incubation parameters helps prevent complications and maximizes hatchling success.

9. **Parental Care:** Snake species display varying levels of parental care. Some may abandon eggs or neonates shortly after laying or birth, while others may remain with their young for a period of time. Understanding the parental care behaviors of the target species is essential for providing appropriate care.

10. **Genetic Diversity and Lineage Tracking:** Maintaining genetic diversity is crucial for the long-term health of captive snake populations. Proper record-keeping, pedigree tracking, and responsible

breeding practices help prevent inbreeding and ensure the preservation of diverse gene pools.

11. **Conservation Significance:** Snake farms play a vital role in conserving and protecting snake species, particularly those that are threatened or endangered. Responsible breeding efforts contribute to maintaining healthy populations, genetic diversity, and potentially reintroducing individuals into their native habitats.

Breeding Strategies and Pairing of Snakes

Breeding snakes on a snake farm involves careful planning, meticulous selection of breeding pairs, and proper management to ensure successful reproduction and the production of healthy offspring. Snake breeders employ various strategies and considerations to maximize genetic diversity, produce desirable morphs, and contribute to the conservation of rare or endangered species. This comprehensive content delves into the key aspects of breeding strategies and pairing of snakes on a snake farm.

1. Selection of Breeding Pairs:

- **Genetic Diversity:** Snake breeders aim to maintain and improve the genetic diversity of their breeding population. Inbreeding can lead to genetic defects and health issues in offspring. Hence, breeders must avoid mating closely related snakes.

- **Desired Traits:** Breeders often pair snakes with desirable morphological traits, color patterns, and genetic mutations to produce visually appealing offspring, which can command higher prices in the market.

- **Health and Age:** Selecting healthy and sexually mature snakes is crucial. Breeding snakes too young or too old can lead to complications during reproduction and increased mortality rates.

- **Compatibility:** Consider the size and temperament of potential breeding pairs to prevent aggression or injury during mating.

2. Reproductive Timing:

- **Seasonality:** Many snake species have specific breeding seasons influenced by temperature and photoperiod. Snake breeders may manipulate these factors in controlled environments to induce breeding outside the natural breeding window.

- **Cooling Period:** Some snakes require a cooling period (brumation) to stimulate reproductive behavior. Breeders carefully regulate temperature and photoperiod to mimic natural conditions and encourage breeding.

3. **Environmental Conditions:**

- **Nesting Substrate:** Provide appropriate nesting substrates and hiding spots for gravid females to lay their eggs. The substrate should retain moisture and mimic the natural nesting environment.

- **Temperature and Humidity:** Maintain optimal temperature and humidity levels in the enclosure to support egg development and incubation.

- **Incubation:** Depending on the species, snake eggs may require specific incubation conditions, such as temperature and humidity. Proper incubation is essential for healthy embryo development.

4. Assisted Reproductive Techniques:

- **Artificial Insemination:** In some cases, artificial insemination may be employed to ensure successful fertilization, especially if natural mating proves challenging.

- **Hatchling Incubation:** Breeders may experiment with different incubation techniques, such as diapause or temperature manipulation, to enhance hatching success rates.

5. Conservation Considerations:

- **Endangered Species:** Snake farms can play a role in conserving endangered snake species by breeding them in captivity and reducing pressure on wild populations.

- **Release Programs:** In collaboration with conservation organizations, snake farms may participate in release programs to reintroduce captive-bred snakes into their native habitats.

6. Record Keeping and Documentation:

- **Accurate Records:** Maintain detailed records of breeding attempts, pairings, dates, and outcomes. This data helps snake breeders refine their strategies and make informed decisions for future pairings.

7. **Market Demand and Ethical Considerations:**
- **Ethical Breeding:** Snake breeders should prioritize the health and well-being of the animals and adhere to ethical breeding practices.
- **Market Trends:** Stay informed about market trends and demand for different snake species and morphs to make informed decisions about breeding priorities.

.

Managing Eggs and Incubation

Running a successful snake farm involves various crucial aspects, and one of them is effectively managing snake eggs and their incubation. Proper egg management and incubation are essential to ensure the health, development, and survival of snake embryos. In this comprehensive guide, we will delve into the key steps and considerations for managing eggs and incubation on a snake farm.

1. **Egg Collection and Handling:**
- Regularly inspect snake enclosures to locate and collect eggs.
- Use appropriate tools, such as tongs or gloves, to gently remove eggs without damaging them.
- Handle eggs with extreme care to avoid jostling or rotating them, as this can harm the developing embryos.
- Record essential information for each clutch, including the species, date of collection, and clutch size.

2. **Incubation Environment:**
- Choose a dedicated incubation chamber with controlled temperature and humidity levels.
- Temperature plays a vital role in determining the sex of snake offspring in some species, so understanding temperature-dependent sex determination (TSD) is crucial.

- Maintain proper ventilation to prevent the buildup of harmful gasses, ensuring a healthy incubation environment.

- Regularly monitor and adjust temperature and humidity settings to mimic the natural conditions of the species being incubated.

3. Incubation Substrates:

- Select appropriate incubation substrates based on the specific requirements of the snake species.

- Common substrates include vermiculite, perlite, and sphagnum moss. Each substrate has its own moisture retention properties.

- Ensure the substrate is evenly moistened, preventing dehydration or overhydration of the eggs.

4. Egg Positioning and Rotation:

- Place eggs in the incubation substrate in the same orientation as they were laid to prevent developmental issues.

- Some experts recommend rotating eggs periodically to prevent adhesion to the shell membranes and improve embryo development.

5. Monitoring and Maintenance:

- Regularly check on the incubating eggs to monitor their progress and health.
- Discard any eggs showing signs of mold, fungal growth, or visible defects to prevent contamination.
- Maintain a detailed record of temperature, humidity, and any observations made during the incubation period.

6. **Hatching and Post-Incubation Care:**
- As the eggs approach their expected hatch date, be vigilant for signs of hatching, such as piping (the first hole in the eggshell).
- Allow hatchlings to emerge from their eggs naturally, avoiding the temptation to assist in hatching unless absolutely necessary.
- Transfer hatchlings to separate enclosures with appropriate environmental conditions for their species.

7. **Record Keeping and Data Analysis:**
- Keep comprehensive records of all incubation-related data, including clutch size, incubation

temperature, humidity levels, and hatching success rates.

- Analyze your data over time to identify trends, make improvements to your incubation protocols, and enhance the overall management of your snake farm.

Caring for Snake Hatchlings

Rearing snake hatchlings on a snake farm requires careful attention to their specific needs, ensuring their healthy growth and development. Snake hatchlings are delicate and vulnerable, and providing proper care is essential for their survival. In this comprehensive guide, we will explore the key aspects of caring for snake hatchlings on a snake farm.

1. **Enclosure Setup:**

- Choose appropriately sized enclosures based on the size and species of the hatchlings.

- Provide secure enclosures that prevent escapes and protect hatchlings from potential predators.

- Use substrates suitable for the species, ensuring comfort and facilitating natural behaviors.

- Include hiding spots, such as small caves or foliage, to reduce stress and promote a sense of security.

2. **Temperature and Humidity:**

- Research the temperature and humidity requirements of the specific snake species to replicate their natural habitat.

- Use thermostat-controlled heating elements to maintain a consistent and appropriate temperature gradient within the enclosure.

- Monitor humidity levels closely, as improper humidity can lead to issues such as dehydration or respiratory problems.

3. **Feeding:**

- Identify the preferred prey items for the snake species and hatchling size.
- Offer appropriately sized, live or pre-killed prey that matches the hatchling's girth or slightly larger.
- Follow a regular feeding schedule, adjusting portion sizes as hatchlings grow.
- Observe feeding behaviors and ensure all hatchlings are consuming food.

4. Hydration:
- Provide a shallow water dish that is easily accessible to hatchlings for drinking and soaking.
- Clean and replenish the water dish regularly to prevent contamination and maintain hydration.

5. Handling and Stress Reduction:
- Limit handling to essential tasks only, such as cleaning or health assessments.
- Minimize stress by using slow, gentle movements when handling hatchlings.
- Gradually acclimate hatchlings to human presence to reduce their stress response.

6. Health Monitoring:

- Regularly inspect hatchlings for signs of illness, such as lethargy, abnormal shedding, or changes in behavior.
- Quarantine new hatchlings before introducing them to the main collection to prevent the spread of diseases.
- Consult a veterinarian experienced in reptile care if you suspect any health issues.

7. Record Keeping and Growth Tracking:
- Maintain accurate records of each hatchling's origin, date of birth, shedding dates, feeding schedules, and growth milestones.
- Monitor the hatchlings' growth rates and compare them to expected growth patterns for the species.

8. Socialization and Enrichment:
- Consider the social behavior of the species and provide appropriate opportunities for interaction with conspecifics, if applicable.

- Introduce environmental enrichment items, such as branches, climbing structures, and hides, to encourage natural behaviors and mental stimulation.

Caring for snake hatchlings on a snake farm requires a thorough understanding of the specific needs and behaviors of each species. By creating suitable enclosures, maintaining proper temperature and humidity levels, providing appropriate nutrition, minimizing stress, and monitoring health, snake farmers can ensure the successful rearing of hatchlings. Proper care not only contributes to the health and well-being of the hatchlings but also plays a crucial role in the conservation and sustainability of snake populations in captivity.

CONCLUSION:

In Part 1 of this book, we embarked on an immersive exploration of the intricate art and science behind snake farming. We delved into the intricacies of snake husbandry, uncovering the secrets of successful breeding programs, ethical practices, and the vital role these reptiles play in both ecology and industry. The overwhelming response from readers and enthusiasts alike has been heartwarming, and we are immensely grateful for your support.

However, our journey is far from over. "Serpents Husbandry: A Comprehensive Guide to Snake Farming - Part 2" promises an even deeper dive into the multifaceted world of snake farming. Prepare to be captivated once again as we unveil a trove of new insights, compelling narratives, and groundbreaking advancements that are shaping the future of this fascinating industry.

What Awaits You in Part 2:

1. **Innovations in Snake Breeding:** Part 2 will take you on a mesmerizing journey through the cutting-edge techniques and innovations that are revolutionizing snake breeding. Discover the latest

breakthroughs in genetics, reproduction, and selective breeding that are leading to the creation of stunning morphs and the preservation of endangered species.

2. **Snake Farming Sustainability:** Join us as we explore the vital intersection of snake farming and conservation. Learn about sustainable practices, habitat protection, and collaborative efforts that are ensuring the survival of both snake populations and their ecosystems.

3. **Venomous Ventures:** Part 2 will shed light on the riveting world of venom extraction and the production of life-saving antivenoms. Explore the meticulous process behind venom collection, the crucial role of snake farms in medical research, and the heroes dedicated to protecting human lives.

4. **Global Perspectives:** Embark on a global odyssey as we traverse continents to unveil the diverse practices, challenges, and triumphs of snake farming in different regions. From Asia to the Americas, immerse yourself in the rich tapestry of

cultures and traditions that intersect with snake farming.

5. **Community of Enthusiasts:** Part 2 celebrates the passionate community of snake enthusiasts, researchers, and farmers. Dive into heartwarming stories that highlight the dedication, camaraderie, and shared commitment to understanding and conserving these enigmatic creatures.

As the anticipation builds for the release of "Serpent Husbandry: A Comprehensive Guide to Snake Farming - Book 2," we invite you to once again become a part of our journey. Whether you're a dedicated snake enthusiast, a curious reader, or someone intrigued by the captivating world of reptiles, Part 2 promises an unforgettable continuation of our exploration.

Warm regards,